Making the Most *of your* Llama

Dr. Linda Beattie

KOPACETIC INK

© 1998 BY LINDA C BEATTIE

First Printing September 1987
Published and distributed in the United States by:
Kopacetic inK, P O Box 323, Kalama, WA 98625
    (360) 673-1743 (fax) or email books@kalama.com

Edited by: Kathryn Doll
Cover Illustration by: Araneen Witmer
Sketches by: Cathy Crisman

Library of Congress Catalog Card Number: 98-067195

ISBN 0-9619634-1-7

Second Edition
First Printing, August 1998
Second Printing, April 2003

Printed in the United States America
Gorham Printing, Rochester, Washington

I wish to thank Dr. A. J. Plummer and all the llama owners past and present, who assisted in rewriting MAKING THE MOST OF YOUR LLAMA.

A special thanks to Cathy Crisman who gave impetus for the first edition and Richard Inlow who shared his llama breeding farm, his knowledge and his life with me.

Table of Contents

Introduction

Making the Most of Your Llama attempts to prepare the farm and the new owner for the llama(s) by offering some suggestions related to housing, health, management and training. The reader is encouraged to write in the book, take it to the barn and add pertinent information related to his or her geographic location.

Making the Most of Your Llama answers some of the frequently asked questions by the curious, the browser, the prospective buyer and the new owner. The information herein comes from respected owners, veterinarians and textbooks related to this unique and lovable creature.

Although much of the information in this book is pertinent to *any* llama and reference is made to breeding llamas and caring for the cria, the primary focus of this book is on the *working llama*. A working llama packs or pulls cart.

1
Getting Ready

Before you bring home your first llama, educate yourself about the animal's needs and ready your farm accordingly. Fence the pasture area, have an adequate shelter from inclement conditions, plan safe transportation from the place of purchase, know the llama's nutritional needs and select a veterinarian who can treat llamas.

Fencing

Fencing is of major importance with any livestock. Give special consideration when fencing for llamas. Barbed wire may be a fence of choice for some types of livestock; it is not the best choice for llamas. Barbed wire will pull out the wool and cut the ears, face and legs of these beautiful creatures. Barbed wire will keep llamas in a pasture, but will not keep predators out.

Domestic dog attack is a major concern. Dogs have done extensive damage to llama herds nationally. Since the llama's fighting fangs are often removed for herd protection, the llama has lost part of its ability to defend itself. Although instinctually the llama will run—there is little room in a fenced pasture. So the first priority in fencing—*keep dogs out.*

A wooden rail fence is aesthetically pleasing and pretty in a pastoral scene. The fence is strong and sturdy. The corner posts do not require cement. The fence should last for at least 20 years. However, by itself it does not deter dogs and other predators neither does it confine weaning cria[1] to a particular location. The owner may want to consider attaching a low and/or high electric wire.

Field fencing or chain link fencing prevents the predator's ability to get in and attack, maim or kill the llamas. An owner must maintain a watchful surveillance of the fencing, being mindful of predators digging under it.

Field fencing inhibits possible unsightly damage to the llamas' ears or wounds that abscess which are often created by razor sharp barbed wire. Llamas can not easily reach through field fencing. The corner posts of field fencing must be well set. The lifetime of the fence is only limited to the wooden posts used.

A 48 inch high field fence with an extra strand of wire or a 2 x 6 inch board at the top will provide an adequate fence.

Chain link fencing offers another alternative. An added top rail greatly adds to its strength. The corner posts need not be set in cement. Its life expectancy is 15 to 20 years. It may also be difficult to install over rough terrain. The cost may also be prohibitive depending on the area.

Other types of fencing include Shire Horse Fence Clip system, Kiwi Fence Rail of New Zealand and PVC rail fencing.

Llamas can jump amazing heights. Normally llamas do not jump fences. They will jump a fence if the animal is being pursued, has a lack of feed, or open females are too close to a stud's pen.

Fencing adds value and beauty to the property as well as protection for the animals.

Housing

Llamas do need to get out of inclement weather. Their long

---

[1] Cria is a baby llama.

wooly coat does not make them invincible to intemperate weather. Adequate lodging prevents llamas from developing rain rot, frost bitten ears, or dying from hyper or hypothermia. Llamas are normally healthy if the owner provides for their basic needs.

Shelters may be as simple as a canvas tent, a typical pole barn, or a complex elaborate structure complete with foreman's quarters. Most llama owners use a pole barn. Besides providing sanctuary for the animals they use the barn to store hay, tack, carts, and feed. Some have a large dry area in the barn used for training or grooming. A few shelters provide a creep feeder for the young cria to eat without being in competition with the adults. Different size animals have different nutritional requirements.

Large farms often have smaller shelters in the field to provide shade, shelter and feeding stations.

Whether llamas are required to pack, be pets, or breed, a "catch pen" in the field or shelter area saves time and energy. This is a small area where llamas come to feed. Use a particular sound like shaking the feed bucket, a whistle, or bell to call the llamas into the area. Consistently reward them for coming.

The catch pen provides the owner with a strong physical advantage in catching the animal for training, grooming, or health care. Keep in mind a full grown llama is stronger and faster, usually taller, and outweighs humans.

Food

The llama is a browser. He enjoys a variety of grass, bark, leaves and brush in his diet. Unlike livestock who graze solely on grass, a llama samples all the delicacies his pasture offers.

The consensus of veterinarians on nutrition indicates an attempt to stick with nature's pattern. Try to provide what they would eat in the wild or by choice. If a llama does not chew on hard substances, its teeth grow too long. In the Northwest many pastures naturally include a ready supply of blackberries, alders, birch, fir and a constant supply of water. Consider adding selenium trace salt with minerals to their diet in granular or block form.

Consider giving the llama free choice[2] good grass hay all winter as a supplement. Ideally the hay should be a high protein hay, cut at optimum season and stored without being rained on to avoid mold. The lush tall green winter grass has no nutritional value and could starve the llama without necessary supplements.

In some areas quality grass hay is not available. Alfalfa hay serves as the main feed. When using alfalfa be sure the animal consumes both stock and leaves. Llamas need an adequate supply of fiber in their diet. Llamas are very efficient ruminants. If moving a llama from grass hay to alfalfa—adjust their diet slowly.

New llama owners can accidentally kill their new pets with a radical change in diet. Upon acquiring the llama, request feed directly from the breeder. Should the diet need to be changed to fit your farm and area make it a gradual process.

In addition to the hay consider adding a llama research grain supplement. With the growing population of llamas several feed companies offer specific grain feeds. Control the amount of grain given to the llama. A llama will eat whatever is provided. Too much grain may cause unnecessary weight gain, bloating and in extreme cases death.

Knowing the weight of a llama assists in administering vaccinations, monitoring feed intake and in general good health. Llama scales are available. Some owners use truck scales to weigh the llamas.

Do not judge the animals weight or fat content by looks alone. The wool hides the actual size of the llama. If in doubt take a picture of the animal dry, then wet. Note the difference. Since many owners are shearing their llamas it is easier to visually observe the animal's physique.

---

[2] *Free choice means the animal can eat its fill of the hay, grass or grain*

If unsure about the nutrition and adequacy of the llama's diet, check with a llama veterinarian.

In 1994 in the Northwest it cost an average of $350 per year to feed and maintain a healthy llama.

Transportation

Llamas can be flown, shipped, freighted, driven in vans, cars, pickups or hauled in various types of trailers.

Each year across the nation ranchers lose a substantial number of livestock due to drastic changes in weather. The same life-threatening weather conditions can be duplicated by llama trailers. In the winter an open trailer can produce temperatures which plunge well below zero.

In the summer a closed trailer can cause blindness and death. Use common sense when transporting an animal. Do not submit the animal to conditions a human could not withstand. When planning to purchase a llama, consider carefully how it will be transported.

If using a trailer try to select a dual-tandem wheeled trailer which will serve your geographic location and time of year. A covered trailer can produce shade in the summer and shelter from rain or snow in winter. Should you own an open trailer, take time to secure a tarp for inclement weather. Some trailers come equipped with removable panels.

Hypo- and Hyperthermic Conditions

Nature at her worst can be harsh. Consider the wind force. The Beaufort Wind Scale lists a whole gale at 55–63 mph. A wind of this force uproots trees and causes major destruction. Hurricane winds began at 74 mph. An automobile or truck easily drives these speeds. Transporting animals in open trailers at these speeds in the winter creates a wind chill factor.

		TEMPERATURE/DEGREES FAHRENHEIT			
		30°	25°	10°	0°
	5	27°	21°	-7°	-16°
	10	16°	9°	-9°	-22°
	15	11°	1°	-18°	-33°
WINDSPEED MPH	20	3°	-4°	-24°	-40°
	25	0°	-7°	-29°	-45°
	30	-2°	-11°	-33°	-49°
	40	-4°	-15°	-36°	-54°
	50	-7°	-17°	-38°	-56°

Estimate the wind chill factor using the above chart. Protect the llama against the weather.

In hot climates, owners may choose to travel at night or early in the morning to prevent hyperthermia. Hyperthermia is an elevation of body temperature above the normal range of 99° - 101.8° Fahrenheit. To monitor the llama in route use a rectal thermometer keeping it in position for three minutes. Electrolyte replacement in the animal's water prior to the trip may be beneficial. Shade and circulating air help. Offer water frequently.

Llamas are subject to the laws of nature. Consider the animal's safety before transporting. Know what abrupt weather conditions can do to the animal's health and welfare. Although cute, cuddly and wooly creatures, llamas are not indestructible.

2
Choosing Your Llama

A domesticated beast of burden for more than 6000 years, the lama species including the yama llama, guanaco, alpaca and vicuna is native to South America.

As the largest llama, about six feet when fully grown, the yama llama is the most suited for packing. This traditional packer weighs about 400 pounds when fully grown. Most yama llama are white with spots or blankets in various shades of brown and black.

The yama llama's cousin, the guanaco, is a bit smaller in stature. Guanacos have exhibited a rather feisty temperament for some owners. Guanacos traditionally have a reddish brown body, white belly, and gray face. Cross breeding between yama llama and guanacos produce smaller versions of the yama llama. They can make fine packers depending on the size and confirmation of the animal. Although less expensive than yama llamas or guanaco crosses, a full guanaco may not be the best choice for a packing animal.

The fully grown alpaca stands about four feet at the shoulder. Traditionally known for its wool production, the alpaca makes a poor pack animal. The wool grows rapidly—often to the ground. Their size prohibits them as a preferred choice for packing in North America.

The vicuna, smallest of the lama species, is on the endangered species list. Unsuccessful attempts have been made to raise the vicuna outside of South America. The extremely soft fine wool or anything made from the vicuna is illegal to possess.

In choosing your llama, be sure his form—size, weight, balance— fits your desired function for him.

Conformation

Conformation is defined as the proportionate shape or contour of an animal. When a llama is observed, the body parts should fit together. Within all body shapes and sizes there should be balance. Conformation is an important issue when selecting a working llama. Observe many llamas. Closely examine the llama's proportions, size, wool and personality before you buy.

A packing llama needs substantial legs. His legs should be relatively straight with forward facing toes. His rear legs as viewed from the side should be directly under him, not camped out or under. His back should be relatively straight. He should not be sickle hocked, swayback or humpback.

The llama's gait should be smooth when walking. His knees should not bang together as he walks. He should not paddle his feet or be down on his hocks. Any of these conditions are considered major defects. Look for them when you purchase a working llama.

In 1986 *Llama* magazine published Dr. Murray Fowler's article, "Form, Function, Conformation and Soundness" in their November/December issue. The article shares detailed charts and diagrams to better understand the llama's body.

Knowing even a little about conformation can be the difference between purchasing a marvelous packer or an early retired pet. One inexperienced buyer purchased what she considered to be a fabulous animal. He could pull cart, was saddle broken and an experienced packer. A year after her purchase the four year old had to be put down for an uncorrectable painful bone problem in his lower legs.

To avoid a similar calamity, an inexperienced buyer should do at least one of the following:

1. Have a pre-purchase exam by qualified veterinarian: this is a standard practice in other animal markets when large prices are involved.

2. Have a pre-purchase exam by you.

3. Buy from a reputable dealer or experienced owner/ breeder.

4. Bring a friend who knows animal conformation, perhaps a horse person.

The purchase of a llama usually requires a substantial monetary investment. To best protect your interest ask for a veterinarian to examine the animal. To enhance the possibilities of purchasing a sound animal, find a breeder who provides proper medical care and who has had some preliminary training with the llama.

Caveat emptor, buyer beware, rings true when purchasing llamas. Never buy a llama you can not touch or examine. The llama's wool may be hiding some flaws which could limit his service to you. Take an inspection check list with you when you begin your search.

Sample Llama Inspection Sheet

Name of farm _____

Identification:

NAME _____AGE _____ SEX ___

WEIGHT _____ (actual or estimated)

REGISTRATION NUMBER_____

COLOR/MARKINGS _____

SIRE _____

DAM_____

Visual Inspection:

Is llama nervous? _____
Broad chest? _____
Normal size for age? _____
Body proportionate? _____

| *Body Conformation:* | Fat? _____ Thin?_____ |
| | Tall?_____ Short?_____ |

Straight back? _____
Leg Conformation:

Forelimb	(front view)	Straight?_____	Curved? _____
	(side view)	Straight?_____	Bent?_____
Hindlimb	(front view)	Straight?_____	Curved? _____
	(side view)	Straight?_____	Bent? _____

Does the llama move freely? _____

Is there lameness? _____

Wool Coat: _____ Uniform?   _____ Patchy?

_____ Length?   _____ Foreign matter?

_____ Crusts or sores?

Vital Signs

Temperature? _____   *Normal 99° - 102°.5 F*

Pulse rate? _____   *Normal 60 - 99 beats per minute*

Respiratory rate? _____   *Normal 10 to 30 per minute*

Fecal pellets normal? _____

Closer Inspection

Evidence of external parasites? _____

Skin look healthy? _____

Male: Intact or gelded? _____

Female: Vulva normal? _____ Any discharge? _____

Check for body fat.   Can you press on the spine?

Large, medium or fine boned? _____

Mouth Area: Sores?_____ Runny nose? _____

Drooling?_____ Scars?_____

Teeth Missing? _____ Fighting fangs?_____

Ears and Eyes: Pupils responsive? _____ Normal eyelid _____

Cornea clear?_____ Cataracts?_____

Any discharge in ear? ____ Ear movement okay? ___

Limbs (check if okay):

	Visual	Palpitation	Nail	Pad
Left Forelimb				
Right Forelimb				
Left Hindlimb				
Right Hindlimb				

Personal Comments: _____

_____

_____

Examination of current owner's medical charts:
>Worming?
>Medicine administered?
>Vaccines administered?
>Current diet?

Be observant of your animal's habits once at home. He may have a particular resting place during a special time of day or stand certain hours of the day or night. Monitor his eating and elimination habits. Should any of these or a combination thereof begin to shift and change, your animal may be ill. Llamas are stoic to pain.

One owner observed her llama limping. The veterinarian and owner witnessed only a minor laceration. It was not until a few days later, the limping having continued, the owner and veterinarian became aware of a 2 inch piece of glass working its way out of the llama's foot. When a change in behavior occurs, be attentive to your llama's needs.

Geld or not?

Gelding is a matter of personal preference. Some owners have regretted their decision. Intact males seem to be in better physical shape. They run and wrestle more in the field than the geldings. Unlike other species, e.g., cows or horses which can cause problems if not gelded, intact llamas usually do not.

If possible, discuss the matter with other owners or commercial packers before you decide. If you elect to geld, the recommended age is between 18 and 24 months.

If you are planning to work your llama, ask to see the animal in action. Sometimes a "packing llama" may only have experienced packing in the pen. Look for evidence of his performance in photographs or on video tapes.

Be an informed buyer; work the llama you are considering for your farm. What kind of temperament does he exhibit? Does he walk with you or need to be pulled? Does he load easily? Can you touch his body all over? Can you put a pack on his back?

Each llama, gelded or intact, has a unique personality and temperament. Llamas by nature want to serve. If you examine and work with the animal prior to purchase he should live up to your expectations.

Additional Help

Locating a breeder who is intent on maintaining healthy llamas, has complete medical records and writes down the genetic practices of his farm adds confidence to the purchase.

The Llama Association of North America (LANA) sponsors seminars throughout the country. Through LANA owners have access to the latest breeding, nutritional, genetic and disease information. LANA invites well-known breeders owners and veterinarians to participate in their symposiums, panels and daily workshops. For more information write to:

> Llama Association Of North America
> 1800 S. Obenchain Rd
> Eagle Point, Oregon 97524-9437
> email LlamaInfo@aol.com

LANA offers some of the best teaching assistance and advice for new owners. Each year LANA sponsors an expo, a national show, and offers a collection of papers to their members.

Heritage

Randolph Hearst brought most of the first personally owned llamas to this country in the early 1920's. Due to strict importation rulings, his animals are the ancestors to the majority of llamas in North American.

As with any species, inbreeding creates serious deformities. Be aware of your llama's lineage. Try to trace information relating to the grandparents and siblings.

When you choose your llama, look for the family's hereditary traits, including birth defects. Not all birth defects are hereditary, but many are. The defect is passed through the line as a recessive or dominant trait.

The research on llama heredity is not a very sophisticated science. Through organizations like LANA and the International Lama Registry, hereditary defects are beginning to be documented.

Llama breeders need to recognize known congenital defects. Your initial examination of the llama checks for some of these defects.

Some of the conditions are known as "lethal traits." The infant dies without surgical intervention, e.g., *choanal artresia* (obstruction between nasal cavity and throat) or *atresia ani* (obstruction of rectum). Some conditions such as protrusion of the lower jaw, failure of testicles to descend, pose little threat to the life of the llama. Some, e.g., an umbilical hernia, may even correct themselves over time.

Hereditary Disorders

SKELETAL: Extra toes, fused toes, bowed knees, dislocated knee cap, twisted neck

CARDIOVASCULAR: Failure of a fetal vessel to close at time of birth, a hole between chambers of the heart, complex anatomical problems

EYE: Cataract, failure of eyelid to develop, blindness

HEAD: Failure of development of the cerebellum of the brain, lack of nasal cavity and turbinate bones, choanal artresia, pro-

trusion of the lower jaw, excessive water on brain, cleft palate, lack of development of palate or of the soft palate
REPRODUCTIVE TRACT: Failure of testicles(s) to drop to scrotum, immature testicle, imperforated hymen, failure of vagina to form, immature ovary, follicular cysts, both male and female organs present in same animal
MISCELLANEOUS: single kidney, atresia ani, failure of diaphragm to form, umbilical hernia

Hereditary disorders may produce a variety of subtle effects, including prevention of conception, fetal death and spontaneous abortion, congenital nonlethal anomalies. Some of these conditions may occur later in life. A brief history of other siblings, aunts or uncles inform you about possible later defects.

Only a few hereditary diseases are documented. Incomplete post mortems, non-reported defects and an insufficient number of animals have hindered identification of conditions as hereditary.

Most of the hereditary defects known are present in other ruminant and domestic animals. The majority of the deformities will probably be documented as recessive traits.

Good breeders pay attention to breeding practices and register births. The registry traces and records the genetic line of the animals. Try to locate owners who register or keep track of their animal's heritage.

Color

Color, although hereditary, should be one of the last considerations when choosing a working llama. In order of importance look for:

1. Conformation
2. Soundness
3. Disposition
4. Color and Type of Wool

Historically color and length of wool dictate price. White llamas are less expensive although the quality and utility of the animals may be par or better than their colored siblings.

Those who buy emotionally, e.g., based on color or whim, ignoring important items such as short wool, spindly legs, or skittish temperament pay dearly later.

No llama has all positive traits; know what is important to you and search for it. Beware of owners who differentiate breeding stock as the "the best" and the leftovers as "packers." It takes a special llama who is built well (conformation) and has a worker mentality[3] to be a packer.

If you are going to train the animal yourself, try to buy at four to five months. Although they can not be used for eighteen months, you will avoid retraining. Like other livestock, if at all possible begin training at an early age.

If you are inexperienced in training the llama (see Chapter Six), ask the owner to show you his commands. Practice with the animal prior to taking him home. Finding a two year old trained llama with packing experience to purchase is limited.

Once you have purchased your animal, mark him for identification. You may chose an electronic chip or tattoo the ears. This will identify your animal in case of theft or loss on the trail.

YAMA LLAMA

3
Keeping Your Llama Healthy

Once you have purchased a sound healthy llama, a minimum of routine care will keep him in good shape. You need to be aware of necessary vaccinations, the diseases which can affect your animal, as well as how to worm him and groom him.

Vaccinations/Injections

The types of vaccinations and preventive medical injections you use will be determined by the geographic problems in your area or by the problem which affects your llama. The vaccination chart offers a guideline for vaccinating throughout the llama's lifetime. Before vaccinating your animal *check* with your veterinarian.

General Vaccination Schedule

AGE GIVEN	*DRUG*	DOSAGE	SEX
Birth	CDT	1 cc underskin	both
	Vitamin A & D	.5 - 1 cc	
	Tetanus Toxoid[4]	1 cc	
Two Weeks	CDT	1 cc	both
4-6 months	CDT	5 cc	both
	Lepto5	2cc	female
	Tetanus Toxoid	1cc	both
6-8 months	CDT	5 cc	both

[4] *Tetanus Toxoid may be in the clostridial (CDT); do not give additional dosage.*

Lepto 5	2 cc	female
Wormer	based on weight	both

Adult Vaccination Schedule

FREQUENCY	DRUG	DOSAGE	SEX
Yearly	Tetanus Toxoid	1 cc	both
Yearly	7 or 8 Way	5 cc	both
Six months	Lepto 5	2 cc	female
	Wormer	Based on weight	both
3 to 4 months In salt	BOSE/Selenium[5]		

Prior to any vaccination program consult a local knowledgeable veterinarian.

Poisonous Plants

Llamas die from accidental plant poisoning. Beware of common plant life in your area which could be deadly to your animal. The following are just a few of the plants/trees which can cause problems:

	Castor Bean
Black Locust	Purple Foxglove
Wisteria	Rhododendron
Azalea	English Ivy
Yew	Mushrooms - Amanita
Buttercups	Poison Hemlock
Jimson Weed	Water Hemlock
Tansy Ragwort	

For more detailed information contact your local veterinarian or County Extension agent. Mount Lehman Llamas offers a booklet which extensively covers poisonous plants.[6]

---

[5] *BOSE/Selenium may not be safe for pregnant females; check with local veterinarian*
[6] *Mount Lehman Llamas, 29343 Galahad Crescent, R.R. #1, Mount Lehman, B. C. Canada*

Parasitic Problems/Worming

Llama owners should be concerned about parasites. Parasites can cause disabilities and death. To prevent and treat parasites, a regular worming program is vital. The drugs and the frequency of treatment depends on individual ranch circumstances.

Many farms worm on a quarterly basis, alternating products recommended by local veterinarians including PANACUR paste, STRONGID paste, and IVERMECTIN paste wormers. You may take fresh fecal samples to the veterinarian to review. For a minimal fee you will know what kinds of worms affect your animals. If you are considering the purchase of an older llama, check on its health program including worm control.

Liver flukes, a common parasite, have been know to kill llamas. Flukes are ingested via snails in grass or hay in water irrigation ditches or creeks. Once the liver starts to be destroyed infections or disease set in.

Avoid flukes by good pasture management with adequate drainage. If possible keep llamas away from swampy or marshy areas. Check periodically for snails. Destroy any found. Ducks offer good organic control.

Diseases

Any animal is susceptible to disease. Some diseases a llama may contract include: coccidiosis, tetanus, botulism, black leg, malignant edema and enterotoxima. Coccidiosis appears especially on small farms where the animals are confined. Diagnosis is simply and quickly done by veterinarian examination of fecal samples. Treatment is effective if administered soon enough.

The description and treatment of each disease is far too lengthy for this handbook. For treatment contact your local veterinarian. Dr. Murray Fowler, one of the first expert llama veterinarians, has written extensively about disease in llamas. He has done research out of the School of Veterinary Medicine at the University of California in Davis.

Grooming

Training, good health, rapport and workability of your llama begins with good grooming habits. During grooming the llama owner/trainer will be:

- · desensitizing the llama to human touch
- · checking for debris thus avoiding future saddle sores
- · brushing dead wool from llama's coat keeping the body core temperature normal so the llama will be less likely to overheat in a working situation
- · brushing will keep the owner aware of any lice infestation or body infections and keep the wool tangle free
- · able to check for clear eyes and nose
- · able to examine feet for abrasions, cracked pads, split nails, puncture wounds - any of which can cause major problems in the future.

Regular grooming is beneficial as a teaching tool for the llama. Grooming helps build rapport with the animal. The wool by product, depending on its quality, may be used for spinning.

To groom the owner may want to use a special llama chute (many kinds are available) or tie the animal *short* with about a 4 inch slack at nose level. Grooming tools include:

sticker brush - purchased at any feed store
rake - ideal for badly matted wool
scissors - used for cutting small sections of
            extensive matting
shears - electric or manual may be purchased at feed stores

When using the scissors hold the matted wool and cut away from the flesh to the outside of the mat. Brush the remaining wool free.

If the animal has never been brushed and matting is extensive shearing may be the only solution. Most farms shear in late spring or early summer. Many owners only shear the barrel of the animal. Some farms in very warm climates shear routinely as a health measure.

Once mats have been cut away and the animal neatly groomed you may notice a more active life in your llama.

Grooming Guidelines

Make the brushing and grooming enjoyable for both of you.

1. Start brushing gently on the neck. The sticker brush can easily hit the skin on the neck so brush softly here. Speak to the llama. "Good llama" is a positive enforcer.

2. Work down the neck. Do not try to groom him all at once, especially if the wool is a mess.

3. Work down the shoulder, repeating "good llama". *Clean* the brush often.

4. Work slowly down the legs. This sometimes makes the llama 'dance.' Go back up if he is jumpy and work down again and again. Comfort the llama with your words and touch.

5. Do not encourage a part at the top of the back. Brush the back towards the tail. A part on the back fosters debris at skin level which could cause sores to develop when the pack is in place. Debris has a tendency to collect at the junction of the neck and back—laughingly called "the lint trap" at one farm.. Do not try to clean this area all at once. It seems to be

a very sensitive area.

6. Brush with the direction of the wool—*down*. Try to brush all layers, not just the top layer. Consider parting off a small square section. Work from the bottom of the square an inch at a time, brushing the wool clean. Then brushing the next inch of wool clean until the area is clean from the skin out.

7. The underbelly is often full of debris. When grooming gently pull out and up. Many llamas do not appreciate your efforts so do a little at a time being gentle. Encourage the animal often.

8. The area near the tail is very tender. Go easy and use lots of praise.

9. When working on the back legs stand close to the llama with one hand on its back, the other holding the brush. Stay clear of potential kicks by standing at the side of the animal. Insist the llama does not kick. Discipline with a loud verbal "no" followed by a jerk on the halter. Always reprimand kicking, pushing or body slams.

10. Consider giving food treats for positive behavior.

11. As the llama responds with good behavior give him more rope. Your goal may be to groom with no halter or rope. This is possible but will take a few years to master.

Nails

Make nail trimming a part of the grooming process. You may discover some llamas need to have nails trimmed once a year and others every few months. Know your animal.

To trim nails secure the llama so he can not jump. Use either a chute or tie short to the wall. Standing to the side of the llama (facing the rear) take the foot off the floor and into your hand. The soft padding will be facing you. You will notice immediately if the nail is flush with the pad or curling up over and towards it. If it is curling take the nail clippers (available at feed stores) and cut parallel to the pad.

Once the nail is flush to the pad trim the sides of the nail at about a 45° angle. If you cut too close to the quick you may draw blood. Although uncomfortable for the animal it probably will not require medical attention.

However, if you accidentally cut the toe or portion of it off, apply an antibiotic ointment to the area and bandage it securely. Keep the animal stalled for a day or two to avoid infection. Change the dressing daily. If you find evidence of heat or swelling to the injury contact your veterinarian immediately.

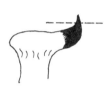 

Cut across then cut diagonally

Teeth

Periodically check your animal's teeth. If too long, the animal may not be getting enough roughage in his diet. Every owner should know the names and locations of the llama's teeth.

During initial inspection of a male llama notice if the fighting fangs have been removed. It has become a standard practice to remove the fighting fangs between 18 to 24 months of age. Notice llamas do not have any bottom front teeth—only a strong mandible.

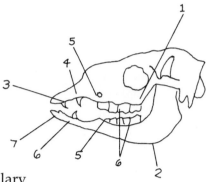

1. Upper jaw / maxillary
2. Lower jaw / mandible
3. Fighting fang / incisor
4. Fighting fag / canine
5. Pre-molar
6. Molars
7. Lower incisors

Consistent grooming is essential in maintaining your animals health and well-being. The process enables you and your animal too become better acquainted and familiar with his strength and increase his workability on your farm.

4
Nutrition

Llamas are ruminants with a three rather than four chamber compartment. Like other ruminants the first compartment is for fermentation which allows the llama to regurgitate and eructate (belch). Studies show llamas to be extremely efficient in utilizing high fiber and poorer quality forage. Despite their efficiency llamas should have quality feed.

Nutritional Needs at Home

Llamas can and will feed on any of the forages fed to cattle, sheep and goats. They may be given alfalfa hay, oat hay, grass hay and most of the concentrates or mixtures of grasses.

Many llamas will subsist on pasturage as long as there is sufficient forage present. In many areas of California, unless a pasture is irrigated it will not provide forage during the summer months. Even in winter when the grass appears lush the nutritional value is nil and supplements may be necessary.

Grain supplements are available for llamas at most local feed stores. Many owners grain their males only during grooming or training exercises. Others prefer to offer about ½ a pound a day for males, one pound or more to pregnant and lactating females with a ½ pound or more free choice grain and alfalfa in the creep feeder per cria (baby llama).

Some owners instead of feeding specific llama grain pellets prefer a mixture of cob and / or alfalfa pellets. Some owners sprinkle a vitamin mineral supplement on the grain.

The majority of llama owners provide the animals with free choice good quality hay. A granulated salt block (12*12*12) is often offered somewhere near the shelter or feeding station.

Llamas will forage on anything in the pasture, so be sure to clean out any poisonous plants.

Simply touching the spine of your animal will give you an indication how it is faring with its diet. Place your thumb and fingers on either side of the spine. Ideally you should feel a nicely padded upside down "V" shape. If it is a pronounced "V" with little "meat" on the bones your animal may be too thin. If you feel a very rounded almost "U" shape you may have an over weight animal. If in doubt always consult your veterinarian.

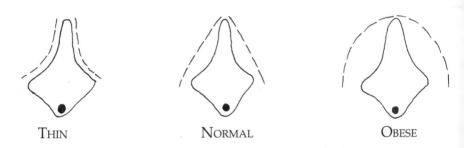

THIN   NORMAL   OBESE

Llamas normally have five to six inches of fat on their belly. Fat works as an insulation. Fat is great during the winter, but can be cumbersome while packing in the summer.

Consistent grooming will also keep you aware of the llama's physical condition. If the wool begins to lack luster, check the diet. The final utilization of protein in the animal's diet goes directly to the wool.

Nutrition On The Trail

Always take supplements on the trail. Anticipate packing one to two pounds of supplement a day per llama, depending on the hiking area. Ideally pick a hike which offers areas for the llama to browse and forage.

Llamas, with their innate curiosity, will attempt to eat almost anything. Know the poisonous plants in the hike area. The County Extension agent, nursery owners, forest rangers, and the local library will help identify poisonous plants.

The research on deadly plants to llamas is incomplete. Assume if the plant is harmful to humans it will harm the animals.

Once the destination is reached allow the llama enough lead rope to nibble a wide area. Tying the llama too short may limit the variety of his diet.

Learn to spot the difference between poisoning and heat exhaustion. The symptoms for both are quite similar, e.g., staggering, white foam at the mouth and/or total collapse.

If you suspect poisoning bring a large branch of the suspect plant to the experts for diagnosis. A leaf or two may not provide enough evidence. As in most cases of poisoning, prevention is the best cure.

5
Breeding & Birthing

Many llama owners, who first purchased a llama for packing, pet or pleasure, later want to breed. Those who choose to breed may be looking for strong pack animals, wooly llamas, particular bloodlines, or color. All who breed should keep conformation as the first priority.

Most veterinarians suggest inbreeding be limited to 25% or less. This is to eliminate potential genetic defects in the cria[7]. Ideally llamas should be breed who are unrelated.

Llamas are spontaneous ovulators. Owners can predict approximately when the cria is due by the date of breeding. With an 11½ month gestation period, if the llama was bred on March 1st and "took", she would ideally deliver around February 14th.

Some llamas are perpetual early birthers—as early as ten months. Others have been known to carry for twelve. Keep records and know your animals.

Breeding Methods

Artificial insemination is not practiced by llama owners. Many farms rely on open pasture breeding or a managed breeding program.

An open pasture breeding program means leaving the stud with one or more females for an extended period of time. The

[7] *What newborn to @ two month old llamas are called*

owner may or may not be able to notice when breeding takes place. This particular method often makes it difficult to know exactly when a cria is expected.

In the managed breeding program the owner introduces the stud to the female at a select time—usually in a controlled environment such as a catch pen or small field. The owner notes if the llama is bred.

Usually the stud is introduced over a period of a week. Ideally at the end of that time period the female will be very unwilling to be bred; exhibiting much spitting and disdain at the male. The male also will not exhibit much interest.

Many farms using this method separate them for at least two weeks, then reintroduce the male to the female. If the "greening effect" is still prevalent, chances are she is pregnant.

The most accurate pregnancy test is done by the veterinarian. The veterinarian may use a blood sample or do an ultra sound to check for the cria.

It is not a bad idea to periodically check with either the stud or another male throughout the pregnancy to make sure it was not aborted or absorbed. Research has found, since the female's uterus is split, pregnancies on the left side are more viable than those adhering to the right.

Birthing

So you are going to have a baby. Hopefully you will know approximately when the cria is due. Most births require little assistance. The majority of births have been found to be between the hours of 10:00 AM and 3:00 PM. This seems to be a mother nature's way of preserving the species—allowing the cria to be born during the heat of the day.

You may not notice much change in the female during the pregnancy. Though she will gain weight, unlike smaller animals it is often difficult to tell just "how pregnant" she is. Chances of having twins are rather slim in llamas, so prepare for a single birth.

As the time draws close consider moving her to a birthing pasture or stall area. Many farms wrap the tail to monitor the milk bag and process of dilation. Handle the milk bag gently so the dam is used to you. You may need to assist the newborn in finding the udder for the necessary colostrum.

As the birthing date nears, you may notice the llama lying down more. She may become cranky and irritable around you. Her vulva may become loose and distended just prior to birth. Her small udder will not grow greatly in size; the teats will get a waxy coating.

Llamas often birth standing up. The cria should be born front feet first, followed by the nose and rest of the body. Do not be in a great hurry to get the baby out and on the ground. Letting it hang naturally allows some of the fluids to drain from the lungs.

If you are lucky enough to observe the birth, check to make sure the embryonic sac is broken around the nose.

Once the baby is on ground the mother usually nudges it, hums to it as a means of getting acquainted and communicating. Be sure to allow normal bonding to occur first if there is no emergency, e.g. inclement weather.

If you are present and outside temperature or weather is very cold, you may want to wrap the baby in a towel or blanket and bring it inside to dry off. The mother should *always* be present with you and the cria.

As you dry the cria check for pink healthy gums. The bottom teeth should be breaking through the gumline.

Many farms have a cria care kit handy for when cria are born. The kit should contain at least some of the following items:

CRIA CARE KIT

> *Blankets or towels*—to dry cria off
> *Blow dryer*—especially if cria is born in winter
> *Thermometer*—check for constant temperature 101° - 102° F
> *String and scissors*—to tie off umbilical cord @ 1 inch below navel[8]
> *Iodine*—Dip remaining cord to prevent infection
> *Vaccinations*—See schedule
> *Scale*—Check cria's weight

Once the cria is dried, leave mother and cria alone to get acquainted. The dam may not pass the placenta immediately, but should do so when left alone. *Never* pull the placenta to "help" the mother. When the placenta has passed check to see if it is complete with two 'horns' extending from the main sac. Some farms store it in the barn for a day or two in case of problems with the cria or dam.

Check periodically to see if the cria is up and nursing. The cria should be up and nursing within three hours of delivery.

A strong baby will attempt to get up right away. You may witness a sucking reflex or the tongue flicking in and out in search of a teat. If the cria has not nursed within three hours consider removing the wax plugs from the dam's udder. Smear some of the milk on the bag and put some on the cria's lips. This seems to help the cria locate the bag.

If you have a dam that will not let the cria nurse. Tie her short and help the baby find the udder. Often after the first suckling, the dam is less reticent about letting the cria nurse.

If the temperature or weather is chilly consider putting a child's down vest on the cria for warmth. Other warming garments are ready made llama blankets, a sweater or sleeveless parka. Wearing the garments backwards makes it easy to fasten the snaps or zip.

---

[8] *Chance of excessive bleeding from cord is minimal*

Many farms keep the dam and cria together inside a barn or enclosure for at least 24 hours before releasing the two into the herd.

If you suspect problems e.g. cria not eating, weigh the cria daily. It is a good idea to keep frozen colostrum (goat or llama) and goat's milk on hand in case the cria needs to be fed. It is not uncommon for llama cria to gain ½ to one pound a day.

To facilitate eating grain, llama breeders build a small feeding station accessible only to cria near the primary feeding area. A small opening allows the cria access to alfalfa/hay and grain without competing with the rest of the herd.

This area is also ideal as small catch pen for the owner and cria to get acquainted. Many beginning training sessions e.g. halter training, voice commands, start in this area at about two months of age.

As you get to know your cria never let it push you or bite at buttons. This 'cute behavior' can continue with a 400 pound animal.

Bottle Feeding

Most farms want to avoid bottle fed cria. A bottle fed llama often requires special training and different handling since it imprints on humans as well as llamas.

If you do need to bottle feed, the local veterinarian may suggest a supplement or have you milk the dam. An eight ounce baby bottle with a large X cut in the nipple works well. Hold the bottle at approximate teat high to avoid inhalation problems. Do not hold it up. The cria should empty the bottle quickly. Keep its lips close to the side to provide suction. The cria may try to pull away; he is by nature seeking four teats.

With your finger at the corner of the mouth break the suction to give the cria a breathing break. When the bottle is empty push the cria away gently and leave immediately. Keep human contact to a minimum.

Possible Problems

Call the veterinarian if the cria exhibits any of the following behaviors for an extended period of time:

grinding teeth
failure to nurse
breathing through mouth
inability to stand
inability to maintain body heat
lack of nursing reflex
poor coloration of gums or grayish pink teeth

Do not be alarmed if the cria heads for a corner to nurse. The cria will instinctively head for a dark place to find milk. Experienced mothers will set the baby up, position body and legs and vocally encourage the cria by humming.

Rebreeding

Most breeding farms breed back about two weeks after the cria is born. This may seem a bit soon, but most farms find greater success in rebreeding at this time than waiting. The llama should be clean from all infections prior to breeding. The veterinarian should check for infections as well as examine the condition of the uterus.

A lactating female who is bred back requires more feed to sustain the cria and the new embryo. On farms which breed back at 10 to 14 days the cria is generally weaned at four to five months. The cria should be eating and drinking on its own.

You may note a significant drop in the dam's weight as she sustains a pregnancy and nourishes a cria.

Keeping Records

All llama farms should keep health records on each of their animals. The information should include (at the very least) the vaccination schedule—type, date, amount. Other information to include may be any behavioral changes; training sessions; breeding dates; birthing date, time, weight of cria. Should the llama be sold it will give the new owner adequate information to keep the animal healthy.

6
Training ABC's

Gentle consistent training works well with llamas. You need not hit, cattle prod, whip or beat llamas into learning. Gentle consistent encouragement and a minimum of discipline, e.g., jerk on the halter or kushing[9] will achieve strong and lasting results.

Training Techniques

As the trainer, always allow enough time for the lesson. Gentle training techniques concentrate on positive reinforcement. Desired behavior is rewarded in several ways:

- Verbal—"good llama"
- Physical—positive strokes, gentle petting or patting of the llama
- Food treats, e.g., alfalfa or feed pellets

Always respond to undesired behavior with
- Verbal rebuke—"bad llama"
- Physical and Verbal rebuke—jerk on halter with loud "no"
- Physical—kushing the llama by pulling down on the halter to bring neck and head to ground level. This behavior duplicates the submissive behavior of llamas to each other in

---

[9] *Bringing the llama to a kneeling position*

the field or wild.

The key to training is *consistency*. Always respond to the positive or negative behavior of your llama. In the beginning *over emphasize* your response to the llama's training.

If you speak softly, it may be difficult for the animal to differentiate between positive or negative responses. Do not be afraid to speak up.

Llamas respond to an individuals mood and behavior. Never be in a rush or show high anxiety; the llama may prove more difficult to work with and be uncooperative. Approach and consistently work with your animals in a positive manner.

Catching the Llama

To train the llama the trainer must first catch him. Catching can be a simple process in the field or barn. Having a catch pen (chapter one) alleviates frustration and allows more time to concentrate on the actual training.

Guidelines:

1. Give the verbal command, "stand"
2. Place your arms out away from your sides speaking firmly
3. Move slowly towards the animal. If the animal won't stand force him slowly into a corner of the catch pen or field.
4. Be familiar with the animal's behavior. Does the llama run around, play hard to get? Work accordingly.
5. Speak his name frequently
6. When close, place hand on the back repeating, "good llama"
7. Work hand up towards the neck to halter the animal.

A halter, lead rope and welded rings constitute the training tools. Special llama halters may be purchased through specialty llama stores, many of which advertise in magazines referred at the end of this handbook.

Use a soft eight foot rope during training. The halter should be adjustable and fit securely. The welded rings will be attached to a solid wall.

The halter is the most important piece of your training instruments. It cannot be so snug as to strangle the animal on its cud or cut his face. The halter must not be so loose that the noseband slips down. This will restrict the air passage. Llamas breathe predominantly through their noses.

The halter must be functional, strong and easy to get on and off. Easy handling becomes of utmost importance when out on the trail. The halter must allow the animal enough movement to eat, chew, yawn and be led effectively.

When you begin haltering your llama, train with tighter chin straps until he learns to walk and behave. Give slack as he masters the behavior. This slack for jaw movement becomes imperative when packing with the llama.

Most llama farms leave the halter on only for training purposes. If stored in a dry place the halters will last longer.

Haltering

Haltering enables you to work with the animal, command authority, and lead him easily. There are several ways to halter the animal including gentle haltering, hard to halter and earring method techniques.

If possible begin haltering when the llama is very young. Frequently halter the baby. Use a two way adjustable halter. Always take the halter off when the lesson is over (about five-ten minutes).

When wearing the halter, the llama should learn it is time to work.
Gentle Haltering Technique:
> · Corner the llama with the command, "stand"
> · Place your arm around his neck
> · Have the halter in the ready position
> · Slowly lift the halter up the underside of the llama's neck (he will not be able to see it)
> · Slowly (at first) lift the nose band over the nose and buckle the strap.
> · Work out a proper fit; too tight will cut the llama's skin, too loose and the llama will attempt to brush it off.

The majority of llamas respond to this technique. If the animal becomes jumpy during any part of the haltering, repeat it. You may have a naturally energetic baby. Do not be discouraged; his energy can eventually be an asset for cart pulling or long packing trips.

Hard to Halter Technique:
> · Corner the llama as above with arm around neck
> · Put on loose neck collar (large dog collar)
> · Move collar up neck to below jaw
> · Tighten it, not to the point of choking, but to keep the collar in place.
> · Fasten lead rope to ring on collar.
> · Tie the rope short to high board or post
> · Put arm around head below ears
> · Bring halter up over nose *quickly*
> · Fasten halter
> · Transfer lead rope to halter ring
> · Release the collar

Some trainers leave the neck collar on (loosely—about three fingers can be put under the collar) for a few days during intensive training to maintain their advantage. When leaving a collar or halter on for an extended period of time, the llama can become entangled, injured, damaged, or wear away wool.

Rarely will a well-trained llama be difficult to halter. However head shyness may make even the best trained llama hard to halter. If the above two methods do not produce the desired result, you may want to attempt the earring method. To avoid personal injury, do not try this method alone. Before you use this method watch an experienced trainer.

The earring method takes several practice sessions before the llama will actually reach to have the halter placed on him.

Earring Halter Technique:
· Catch the llama in a small area
· Put arms around neck area, tightly
· Work hand up the neck, grabbing an ear with one hand: llama may lurch and move in circles rapidly
· Twist the ear—not enough to break the cartilage, the llama will stop and stand.
· Bring halter up underneath neck and chin
· Quickly place halter over nose and fasten halter with *one hand* while holding onto ear
· Continue to hold onto ear and touch head, eye and ear area to desensitize head.
· Holding onto ear, unfasten and remove halter
· Repeat on and off process three times
· End lesson on positive note where *you* win
· Reward the llama with food and free time

Rope

A soft nylon eight foot lead rope works well during training and while packing. The rope will not break and serves a variety of functions. Use the rope to lead, pack, tie and as an incentive to walk.

When the llama lies down and refuses to move, take the lead rope and move to the rear of the llama. Tug gently. The llama's head will move towards you. Since this is an uncomfortable position he should stand immediately.

Restraints

Welded rings securely fastened to a solid wall are paramount when the llama becomes more powerful than the trainer. Take five two inch rings attached to a large screw. Place one ring high on the wall about the nose height of a llama; place two about five and a half feet from the floor and two about four and a half feet from the floor (see figure). Secure the screws.

Do your grooming here. In the beginning tie his nose to the upper ring until he behaves by standing still for any process, e.g., brushing nail trimming, medication. As he becomes used to you and the procedures, loosen the lead. If you have a good rapport with the animal you may eventually be able to groom without a rope or halter.

You can build an *economical* restraining chute using a *solid* wall, with a ring at head level and two securely attached rings and two permanently attached straps (see figure). Attach an 8 foot lead rope to the llama's halter.

Slip it through the ring and tie with an knot that can easily be undone. Bring the straps under the llama and tie them so he can not lie down.

A wooden rectangular chute can be purchased or made. The sides are solid plywood. One farm modified the side with a removable panel to allow easier access for nail trimming. One end is entirely open. The other end has two adjustable vertical bars to secure the llama's head. Another farm attached short shelving to the sides to contain grooming, vaccination, tattooing and nail trimming supplies.

Metal chutes are also available for purchase.

Body Language

Llamas have often been called "silent brothers." The llama communicates his needs through intonations (humming) and his body.

Balking, stopping, dragging and suddenly lying down are silent messages that something is wrong. One owner had trained his animal to ride children on his back. The llama consistently worked, drove and rode with no problem. One day the llama, after giving 15 children saddle rides, laid down. He refused to get up. The owner immediately removed the saddle. There was no evidence of a sore. He encouraged the llama into the barn.

Puzzled, the owner called the veterinarian. A physical examination showed a possible blocked bowel. The llama did not respond to treatment. Three days later he died. An autopsy found evidence of a stuck kidney stone and scarring from many others. In spite of pain, the stoic animal gave his best.

As an aside, intact males have a better chance of passing stones than gelded llamas. Geldings have a smaller urinary tract.

Llamas naturally work to please. If your animal suddenly refuses or his behavior alters dramatically, call for assistance.

Training Baby

A newly weaned baby, four to six months old, will learn to trust you implicitly. He responds best to love, positive strokes, and comforting humming sounds.

Keep the baby in close quarters when you begin to work with him You will be able to catch him easily. If possible have an older trained llama near or in the pen with you to assist in the training. The baby, like other animals, learns from mimicking behavior.

Training a llama takes months of consistent workouts. Each time you work with him, play or hike it is a training session.

As the trainer, present an air of confidence, allow enough time for the lesson (at least 10 minutes) and *always* end the lesson with some positive reward.

You are the herdmaster. Although the baby may seem wooly, docile, and cute, he has immense strength. Never sit on the llama to restrain him. One owner sat on a four month old llama to hold him down in order to administer a shot. The moment the needle pricked the skin, the owner found herself across the stall.

Do show him you are the herdmaster. He will recognize your authority by curling his tail up or crouching submissively. Sometimes having an older llama present during training will reinforce this important attitude.

An older llama will demonstrate lack of fear coming to you when you enter the stall, looking for treats, or a positive stroke. At this time encourage the baby to eat out of your hand.

If he refuses your hand, try feeding him with a bucket. In a few days try again to feed from your hand. He will know what to expect and be more obliging. You will have trained him to accept a positive reward.

If feasible, and you have the time, when you catch the baby

halter him. Brush him "gently" a couple of times a day. Get him to trust your touch with the brushing and stoking motions. Brushing him in this manner serves three purposes:

· the llama knows he is caught and can not get away
· it desensitizes the llama for packing and nail trimming
· it provides for healthy wool and a more contented animal

Discover what your animal likes best about you, e.g., cologne, hair shampoo, touching a certain spot on his body or food and use it to your advantage.

Isolation

When a new llama comes to the farm, you may want to isolate that llama from the main herd. The isolation period lets you observe the animal's personality and habits. Isolation protects the llama from a drastic diet change. It can also protect the llama, especially a very young one, from the natural jockeying for position in the herd and allow time for getting acquainted over the fence.

Isolation is a good time to acquaint the animal with other pets and the human family.

Training the Adolescent

If you acquire an adolescent—a llama who is 15 to 24 months old—apply the same training methods. You may have to work longer if he has developed any bad habits. You will have to exert more energy to lead him; he weighs two hundred pounds more than a baby in training.

Combating Negative Behavior

The adolescent may display some negative behavior, e.g., pushing, spitting, or lying down and refusing to move. Should he display any of these behaviors, remind him you are the herdmaster. Insist on proper behavior.

As one bumper sticker reads, *"Spit Happens."* Unless provoked, llamas seldom spit. The llama spits to protect, challenge, or display displeasure.

Your first encounter with spitting will probably be during grooming. Brushing and vaccinations can be painful. The llama should spit at the wall. Do not approve of the llama spitting at you! Respond with a loud and firm ,"no"; consider jerking the halter at the same time. Return to what you were doing, even for a few moments. If you don't, the llama has learned he can stop *your* behavior by spitting.

He may replace spitting with pushing against you. Again respond with a loud and firm, "no", jerk on the halter and continue the activity. If the animal insists on pushing, take precautions for your own safety before you discipline. Eventually the llama will quit. The training may take a few months.

If the llama kicks, the same disciplinary action applies. As the llama submits to your mastery, he may merely move his leg a few inches from the ground and tremble. Reward him for this behavior.

Should an intact llama demonstrate consistently aggressive behavior to you or your herd, you have two choices. Consider removing him from your farm or geld him. Gelding has not always proven to be a successful method to inhibit negative behavior. It may take months and consistent negative reinforcement to make the animal docile.

Lead Training

A llama will let you pull him almost anywhere. Your primary goal will be to have the animal follow you on a loose lead keying in on your shoulder.

The llama will let you drag him all over the pasture. If he drags, jerk on the lead and release. You may have to do this several times before he moves. If he moves a few feet, reward him!

· Voice command—"walk"
· Physical command—pull and release
· Sound command—click your tongue against your cheek.

If the animal is uncertain or balks at following your lead, take the rope and move to the rear of the animal. Since the head is in an uncomfortable position, the body will follow. Continue pulling in this circular movement until the animal will walk in ever widening circles.

Once the animal begins to follow, lead in different directions. Acquaint him with the farm area. Let him experience barking dogs, creeks, rivers, boats, houses, lights, horns, windows, kids, whatever is naturally around your farm. Expose him to as many things as possible.

Each time he encounters a new object and is rewarded with a positive experience, he will be more adept for the unexpected on the trail. The exposure to new things also builds trust between you and your animal.

Consistently reward him for good behavior with verbal praise or alfalfa treats.

Once you feel comfortable with the llama, take him walking in the neighborhood. Again expose him to anything new. Beware of the walking surface. Asphalt can burn the llama's pads. If walking on roadways, walk in the cool of the day.

Voice Commands

Train your llama with voice and physical motion commands. One owner found his curious llamas in his neighbor's field. He simply crossed the road, shouted, "Go home, bad llamas" and pointed home. The llamas, much to the neighbor's surprise, went home.

Talk to your animals. The more they know your voice, the better the will respond to you.

During training you will be using several equestrian terms.

STAND or WHOA: Say it just prior to stopping. Follow with a jerk on the halter to indicate stop. Eventually the animal will stop on voice command alone. "Stand" can also be used when cart pulling or packing an untied llama.

BACK-BACK-BACK: Use this command in tight places, e.g., entering a trailer, packing, loading or while cart pulling.

CLICKING OF TONGUE: Indicates forward movement. Use primarily with cart pulling.

JUMP: Give this command when he must cross a creek or go over a fallen log.

LOAD UP: use with any kind of loading procedure.

COME or COME IN GUYS + WHISTLE: Use to bring animals in from the field to the barn or catchpen area.

RUN + CLICKING OF TONGUE: Use to hasten the llama ,e.g., oncoming cars, crowd control, shows. Adding the clicking sound the llama will have a faster gait; may add to "come" command to speed llamas into barn/catchpen.

WALK: Use for forward motion

KUSH: Traditionally a camel command for lying down. Kush is used for disciplinary action or seating the llama. At first, couple "kush" with pulling straight down on the halter ring, lowering the head to the ground. If the animal resists lying down, "nip" the knees front and back with fingers. Your are imitating a natural dominate behavior in the pasture. The animal will lie down.

GOOD LLAMA: Use as a positive reinforcement. Consider combining with positive stroking or food.

BAD LLAMA: use as negative reinforcement. Shake your finger or jerk on the halter to reinforce your authority.

EASY: Use to calm or slow the animal's gait. Ideal for cart pulling or packing.

KISS or KISSES: Use to encourage friendly identifying gesture; couple with blowing gently in the llama's face.

GOODIES: Use when you have food or treats in hand; the llama once he learns "goodies" will look for them on your person.

PAY ATTENTION: Couple with name of the animal; use when training or in a pack train.

GET IN LINE: Use in the pack train when you want the llama in a straight line.

As you get to know your animals, you may find other words or phrases which work well. The voice commands used must have a unique sound. Do not use a combination such as "whoa" and "go" during training. They are too similar in sound for the llama to decipher these contrary commands.

Training the Adult

Ideally trainers prefer working with animals under two years of age. The adult llama can be trained to your specifications using the same methods described previously.

Usually the untrained adult on your farm will be a female. It will be important for you to work on body desensitization by thorough grooming and consistent, gentle handling. Working with her in this way, you will gain her trust and be able to handle her during birthing or giving inoculations.

Regardless of the llamas' age, each time you approach, talk, stroke, handle or play with them you are participating in the ABC's of training.

7
Llama Packing & Camping

Once you have trained your llama to pack in the backyard, you and he are ready for the first of many 'road tests.' Although you can not predict the weather for an ideal get-away, using the right packing and camping equipment enhances the possibility of an enjoyable time.

Outfitting The Llama

Think *light* when gathering equipment. Several lightweight aluminum llama packs are available.

To pack a llama you will need:

· a lightweight frame: an aluminum frame keeps the 70 to 90
   pound load from shifting
· a chest strap
· a pad: use a rug or carpet piece cut to proper size
· panniers: these may be duffel bags or large day packs[5]

The cost of equipment may range from $140.00 (above) to more than $600.00.

In addition to the llama pack frame include:

· a lightweight tie out rope for each llama
· an extra halter

[5] *Consider sewing shoulder straps to the panniers in case a person must pack them out*

· a 20 foot water-skiing rope with snaps—one per llama
· a llama medical kit
· mole skin
· antibiotic ointment
· 2 inch wrapping tape
· 3 inch medical wrap
· thermometer (to check for hypo/hyperthermia)
· electrolyte replacement for heat stress
· nail clippers
· pain killer
· supplementary food (especially if unsure about foraging area)
· a fifty pound weight scale (fishing type)

A two year old can pack fifty pounds all day. As he gets older and stronger, increase the weight. Even though fifty pounds may not seem like much when you see this towering animal, remember he is young, inexperienced and *still growing*. Avoid future back injuries now by limiting the weight of the pack.

Normally a fully trained adult will carry between 70 and 90 pounds. Pack the panniers at home. Weigh each and distribute according to your animals capability. If you tape a list of contents to the inside of the pannier, once it is packed, repacking on the trail no longer creates frustration.

Pair panniers by weight. They should weigh the same. You may have to add a rock or redistribute the contents to balance.

If possible take an extra llama. If one of your pack animals becomes injured or ill, you will not have to pack out the panniers. If you are limited in the number of llamas, carry an extra empty human backpack in case of an emergency.

Outfitting The Camp & Camper

The day or weekend camper must think and plan *light*. Not

only may the llama be in less than optimal condition from grazing peaceably in the pasture all week, but the owner/trainer may suffer from a lack of conditioning as well.

Depending on the hiking area and weather, consider packing the following for a weekend trip:

down sleeping bag good to -20° F

long-sleeved shirts and T-shirts

extra shoes—tennis

lightweight walking shoes

emergency blanket

lightweight butane stove

lightweight 2 to 4 man tent

small containers of soap and oil

2 extra gas canisters

lightweight cooking utensils

3 pots with clap-on lids

blue ice (stays frozen longer)

water and windproof matches

cushioned foam sleeping pad

small outdoor thermometer

a down vest

ample boot socks

a rain poncho

2 flashlights

back up candles

small butane lantern

extra cord

2 small coolers

garbage sacks

water filter

collapsible bucket

fishing poles

water bottles

ground cloth

towel, cloth and/or paper

Food

Plan to pre-cook most of the menu. If you pack it in frozen, you will have extra 'ice', need limited cooking utensils and save on butane. Freeze butter, bread and popcorn for additional 'ice.'

Take only the food you will use. You may want to consider taking packages of freeze-dried food in case of an emergency stay.

Each hiker should carry a day pack. The day pack will avoid unnecessarily entering the panniers on the trail. Pack cameras, first day's lunch, insect repellant, snack, toilet paper, and a water bottle in a day pack. Leave enough room to store extra clothing as the day warms up.

Always think light; discard duplicated items. Know what weight your llama can comfortably carry. Practice at home. Adjust the pack frame to fit a particular animal. Weigh and assign panniers before you leave. Tape the name of the llama on pannier and a frame to avoid inappropriate weight distribution.

Condition your llamas prior to the packing trip. Three to five days before your intended hike trim the llama's nails. You want no evidence of sores, lacerations, or infection in the foot or leg prior to the hike.

Toughen pads by walking llamas with loaded packs on rocky surfaces.

If you are traveling a long distance, arrive at the trailhead the night before. Your llamas will be fresh and eager to start in the morning. Do your serious packing during the early morning hours, before the sun gets too hot.

Avoid packing in 100° F weather. If it is too warm, your llamas may show signs of heat exhaustion. Should your llama begin to stagger, develop white foam around the mouth, or he collapses, immediately remove packs. Begin applying water to neck, belly and legs. Encourage him to drink water. Use the electrolyte replacement from your llama medical kit. To avoid these serious problems, travel in the cool of the day.

Where to Camp

Contact the Ranger Station or Forest Service in the area you wish to hike. Tell them you have llamas and would like information about trails suitable for pack animals. Ask for a map to help plan your trip. In some areas, because of the llamas popularity and friendly use of the trail, trails forbidden to horses or pack mules are open to llamas.

Make the first hike an easy one. A Ranger or Forestry Service personnel can assist in determining the ease of the trail. Be sure to ask about:

fire conditions
available water
condition of trail
weather
regulations
poisonous plants

Utilize the Ranger Station's services to double check on weather prior to the hike. You can reciprocate by packing out other people's garbage or giving up to date information about the trail once you pack out.

Make your first hike a short distance with low elevation gains.

Ready to Hike

At the trail head unpack the tie out ropes. Tie the llamas close together without entangling the lines. The llamas will naturally huddle together in a strange environment.

Stay within sight and sound of your llamas. Put hay out for the animals; offer water in a bucket if they have not had water from a running stream. Although llamas may not drink readily, consistently offer them water to avoid dehydration.

Keep a flashlight handy to ward off unwanted camp visitors.

Offer water again in the morning. Tie the llamas short to the trailer or tree to load the packs.

Take the appropriate frame and pannier and load the llama. The lightest load goes to the youngest and most inexperienced llama.

On The Trail

Once the llamas are packed, they may start tugging and pulling. The animals are excited and anxious to move out. After fifteen or more minutes on the trail the llamas should settle into a comfortable pace.

Trouble Shooting

If the train moves sluggishly or a llama continues to move out of sequence, you may have placed them in an inordinate manner. Llamas naturally demonstrate dominance and submission. If a young animal, normally submissive, is put at the lead he will show signs of submission by dragging, hesitation or letting you pull him along.

An older llama in a submissive position may start spitting or rebuking the llamas ahead or behind. Stop fighting the system. Rearrange the llamas into their dominant order.

The head llama may halt suddenly on the trail. He is checking on his pack train. He may pause to let others catch up.

If you are at the end of the pack train and need to make a nature stop, your llama may screech at being left behind. When you are ready to move on he may show excessive energy, running to catch up to the pack train.

When an animal suddenly stops, balks, drags or becomes sluggish on the trail, check for the probably cause:

· llama may need to catch his breath—evidenced by flared nostrils. A llama does not normally breathe through its mouth
· scared; young animals especially need reassurance
· 'nature calls'
· halter needs adjusting
· panniers may have shifted, so weight is unbalanced
· wound to pads, feet, or legs

Llamas are sensitive animals. They speak to you with their body language. If a llama absolutely refuses to move and you have checked the probably reasons, examine the trail. One owner nearly walked her pack train into four inch bramble thorns, which could have caused extensive foot injury to the llamas.

If none of the above problems exist move in a different direction for a few minutes. The llama may have seen or smelled something which frightened him. If the animal refuses to move solely due to stubbornness, pinch his rear near the testicles. In nature a dominant llama nips for submission in the same area.

Trail Etiquette

You may not be the only packers using the trail. Backpackers, mules, and horse packs may be on the same trail. Avoid accidents with horseback riders by shouting to identify your presence. Horses may bolt or spill riders if unaware of you and your pack train.

· Move off the trail as much as possible to let others pass. Reassure the horses. Talk to them as they go by.
· Keep the llamas out of snow packs and running streams. They have a tendency to defecate in them. This is an unsanitary practice.
· Advise loose dog owners your animals may attack for fear of being attacked. Ask to have them leashed until you pass by.
· Motorcycles have the right of way. Protect your animals by listening for them and moving off the trail.

At Camp

Attend to your llamas needs first. Give them water. Tie them. Know several tie methods including tie out stakes, tying to rock filled panniers, tying to heavy deadwood, tie three llamas together or tie them to a rope line.

Remove panniers and pack frames. Set up camp.

Depending on their graze, give the llamas grain or a supplement.

Relax and enjoy your time together.

No Trace Camping

Every camper shares the responsibility to preserve and maintain the natural environment. Camping outside established campgrounds, makes your responsibility even greater.

You can minimize your impact on an area using these sixteen steps:

1. Use deadwood on the ground for firewood.
2. Burn in existing fire rings *when* fires are permitted.
3. Stir ashes with water, then bury or spread them.
4. Pack out all leftover food and garbage.
5. Pack out any pre-existing garbage.
6. Camp more than 200 feet from water.
7. Camp in bare spots not on the flowers.
8. Use foam pads for bedding not fir boughs.
9. Wash away from the water source.
10. Chose toilet site away from likely campsite and bury feces and toilet paper.
11. Try to leave the area more pristine than when you arrived.
12. Do not pick the flowers.
13. Hike on existing trails.
14. Use tennis shoes in camp; tennis shoes cause less damage in meadows and wet area.
15. Use highly visible colors on your llamas to avoid mis taken identity with wildlife.
16. Stake llamas in suitable areas, e.g., meadows.

Human Waste

The first six to eight inches of earth is usually rich with biological decomposers. The decomposers break up organic material. Keeping this in mind when camping:

- carry a digging tool
- select a suitable screened spot at least 50 feet from any open water
- dig a hole eight to ten inches in diameter and no deeper
- after use, fill hole with loose soil and tramp on sod
- nature will decompose in a few days.

Animal Waste

Llamas will defecate in the area you choose, if you carry a starter can. Place pellets in an appropriate place to minimize contamination.

Avoid water. Do not let your animal stand in water for extended periods. Running water tends to encourage elimination.

"No trace" camping minimizes the impact of campers and llamas.

Maximizing Enjoyment

Preparation, conditioning, and training create a relaxed environment. To maximize your enjoyment consider this summary of tips for the trail:

- use low use areas
- avoid weekends
- bring food which requires little cooking
- freeze all food to use as ice in coolers
- carry llama feed, extra ropes
- travel in small groups

· stay on the main trail
· walk single file
· take no short cuts
· do not chop standing trees or let the llama eat its bark
· take pictures, not flowers
· avoid campfire, except when permitted
· report significant information to the Ranger Station or
    Forestry Service
· subscribe to a backpacking magazine
· lobby for wise planning of natural parks

Be safe, prepared, and trained. If you ignore any of the three you minimize the chance for a wonderful camping experience.

8
Ground Driving and More

Ground Driving

Once the llama understands and obeys voice commands training may begin for cart pulling or ground driving. One owner has trained a team of ten llamas to pull a wagon. Whatever kind of cart, wagon, or ground driving you elect to do, use an older animal. Beginning too young may cause spinal injury as the animal matures.

Ground driving involves serious training. Mastering the voice commands is paramount to your success. The first lesson your animal must learn is letting you be behind him.

Begin by using the halter and two eight foot lead ropes attached to the center ring of the halter. Start the lesson in the barn or corral area, keeping extra animals and llamas away.

Gently guide the ropes along his back. Use them as reins. Stand behind the llama. He will try to reposition himself behind you. Encourage him to "stand", repeating "good llama." Continue until he accepts your new position.

Once he is comfortable with you behind, click your tongue and say, "walk." You may have to push him slightly in the beginning. You should not fear being kicked if the llama is thoroughly desensitized by grooming.

When he moves one step—*Praise Him.* Usually after three to

five days of fifteen minute sessions he will walk readily in front of you. The fifteen minutes may seem tedious. Pass through them with patience. You are training your llama to respond to something entirely new.

Once you can walk in a small area, move to the corral or field. Practice your voice commands.

Commands

CLICK YOUR TONGUE—forward movement
WHOA—stop
PULL LEFT ON REINS—move to the left
PULL RIGHT ON REINS—move to the right

Always end your training sessions with positive affirmation. If the training has gone well and you have not completed the fifteen minutes end early.

End the lesson in a different place each time. Treat him with a snack, positive stroking or free time.

When the llama has learned the commands move outside a fenced area. Start maneuvering between trees and shrubs. Walk down driveways. Be sure the areas are wide enough for the cart to eventually maneuver through or around. Practice making wide turns as if the cart were behind the llama.

Once the llama masters the art of ground driving he is ready to learn how to pull cart.

Cart Pulling

All of the previous training comes into play as the llama learns to pull cart.

Be sure the harness fits securely. Practice ground driving the llama with the harness. The harness feels different to the animal; he must adjust to it before putting him in front of a cart.

While you work with him in the new harness, keep the cart in the pasture or barn area. The llama's curious nature will encourage him to inspect the foreign object and conquer any fear.

Formally introduce your llama to the cart. Tie him short. Bring the cart around to his side and lay the shafts on his back. Bounce it lightly.

Move the cart around to the other side. Lay the shafts on his back. Bounce the cart again.

Bring the cart behind the llama. Roll it into position. Hook the shaft straps loosely in case you need to remove them quickly. Walk around the llama and the cart. Speak reassuringly.

As you walk around bounce the cart lightly. Simulate the motion of a moving cart. Praise him constantly. Disconnect the straps and conclude the lesson on a positive note.

Do *not* let him pull cart right away. Warm up for cart pulling by practicing with the harness only. Practice starts, stops, turns and backing in the harness.

Use a blanket under harness to protect the wool.

When you first pull cart have two people ready with lead ropes attached to the harness to hold and control the llama's walk. Know instinctively where to disconnect the harness in case of emergency. Carry a knife to cut the harness should he run into extreme difficulty. A frightened llama can injure himself.

Ask a horse trainer for assistance if you have a particular problem. If you do not know a hose trainer, contact the County Extension Office for information or a referral.

Some owners have begun team drive training using the same techniques and patience necessary for cart driving.

Packstring

A successful packstring relies on all previous training. The animals must have a good command of their name, verbal orders, an obstacle course, and be rope wise.

School the animals in the pasture. If your animals have been trained to pack and have been staked out on the trail they are rope wise.

Begin working a packstring with three llamas. The pack frames need to have secure chest straps. Tie the lead llama to the fence. Tie the second llama to the leader's pack frame. Attach the third llama to the second's pack frame using the eight foot lead ropes. Allow a four to five foot spacing between the animals.

In the beginning place the animals in their hierarchical form. As the animals become accustomed to the packstring, alternate positions. Develop a variety of leaders; this becomes necessary if the lead llama is injured during a hike or becomes overly tired.

Should the animals become tangled during the practice session, unsnap the lead rope at the halter. Become adept at preventing and anticipating problems. This is imperative when leading a large packstring.

Allow at least fifteen minutes for the llamas to adjust to the packstring. Pay attention to the packstring. Walk at the same pace. Walk them in a large circle during this 'warm-up' period. For better control, keep close to the fence line. Should an animal get out of line, it is easier for you to pull him back into the string.

If the animal continues to wander, make a sharp hairpin turn towards him; jerk his halter with the verbal command, "get back in line."

Once the animals walk in sync and you feel confident of their latest training, begin maneuvering and weaving them through trees or shrubs. Exaggerate your pattern. With more practice sharpen your path. If you have a packstring with more than three llamas, monitor the position of the end animal. He can easily get hung up.

When they master the maneuvers, you may take them out of

the pasture and onto the obstacle course. Create obstacles which represent nature.

Windfall—fallen logs blocking the trail
Wooden Bridge—duplicates sound and sight
Creek—forage, duplicate running water
Trees—jump over, rather than walk through as with the wind fall
Open Gate—large opening with bar to walk under
Tunnel—if possible

Keep the string moving. Should you work with a four to six string and need to stop, immediately tie the lead and end llamas to avoid entanglement. A second person is invaluable when beginning to train a packstring.

A packstring is an excellent example of demonstrating your llama's training. Consider demonstrating your llama's abilities at fairs, expos or national shows.

Trainer Llama

A trainer llama encourages reprimands and assists in training older llamas. Place the trainer in a lead position, put him through his training with the newcomer behind as in a packstring.

The trainer will not tolerate balking or resistance. He will turn and verbally reprimand. If this does not work, he may turn and physically eschew his authority at his pupil.

You will find the training process of an older llama much easier if you do it in conjunction with a trainer llama. Consider using him when you train younger animals as well. He offers security and models the desired behavior.

4-H

The llama has become a part of the 4-H agricultural program. In the past the Llama Association of North America (LANA) has sponsored 4-H projects. The participants show their llamas at fairs or at special llama events.

Associations

To remain current about the medical, legal and llama industry consider joining any of the following associations. Most publish their own newsletter and may have their own website. Many sponsor llama events or educational programs for owners.

> Alpaca and Llama Show Association, P O Box 1189, Lyons, Colorado 80540, (303) 823-0659
>
> Alpaca Owners & Breeders Association, 1140 Manford Ave., P O Box 1992, Estes Park, Colorado 80517-1992, (970) 586-5357 or fax (970) 586-6685, for information call (800) 213-9522 or e-mail kenaoba@aol.com .
>
> Canadian Lama Association, Hammond Rd., C#8, RR#1, Lumby, British Columbia, Canada VOE 2GO
>
> International Lama Association, 2755 Locust St. #114, Denver, Colorado 80222, 1-800-WHY-LAMA or e-mail intillama@aol.com provides membership directory and yearly llama expos.
>
> Llama Association of North America, 1800 S. , 1800 Obenchain Rd, Eagle Point, Oregon 97524-9437 or llamainfo@aol.com
>
> Natural Fiber Producers Association, Box 292, Sunol, California 94586, (415) 862-2028

Almost every state or region has an association or affiliation for llamas and/or alpaca breeders. Contact the International Lama Association for more regional information.

Additional Resources

Several years ago the Llama Association of North American, the International Lama Association and Richard Patterson (llama breeder) pulled their information and resources to form the International Llama Registry. The merger manifested a single authoritative lama registry. Lama Registry since it incorporates the registration of guanacos, yama llamas and alpacas.

INTERNATIONAL LLAMA REGISTRY, P O Box 8, Kalispell, Montana 59903, (406) 755-3438 or fax (406) 755-3439.

Additional Reading

Since *Making the Most of your Llama* was originally published in 1987 other books have been written about the lamas (yama llama and alpaca). Some of the books are listed below. They may be purchased or ordered through the Llama Store in Jackson, California or your local bookstore.

First Aid for Llamas and Alpacas, by Dr. Murray and Audrey Fowler, available through the Llama Store, 44 Main St., Jackson, California 95642 or 1-800-401-LAMA.

Llamas, Caroline Arnold, Morrow Jr. Books, 1988.

Llamas: An Introduction to Ownership. Caret Hawding, 1991, Alpine Press.

Llamas Are The Ultimate, Doyle Markam, 1992, Snake River Llamas, 7626 406 N. 5th W., Idaho Falls, Idaho 83402 $16.95 includes S/H.

Medicine and Surgery of South American Camelids, first or second editions available Dr. Murray Fowler, 1989, Iowa University Press.

Spinning Llama and Alpaca, Christ Switzer, P O Box 3800, Estes Park, Colorado 80517.

Subscriptions

Many magazines have become available for the llama owner. Many give medical updates regarding the species. Some offer detailed information regarding training, upcoming shows, the results of state fairs and, of course, lamas available for purchase.

Alpacas, Quarterly publication. P O Box 1968, 714 Poyntz Ave., Suite B, Manhatten, Kansas 66502, (913) 537-6109 fax.

Back Country Llama, 2857 Rose Valley Loop, Kelso, Washington 98626, (360) 425-6495 or fax (360) 577-2803 or e-mail llamapacker @kalama.com

Llama Banner, bi-monthly publication, P O Box 1968, Manhatten, Kansas 66502, (913) 537-6109 fax or (913) 537-0320. Articles, detailed information regarding sales and shows in United States, various state maps of owners.

Llama Life II, Quarterly news and views publication. 5232 Blenheim Rd, Charlottesville, Virginia 22902, (804) 286-2288 or fax (804) 286-4983 or lamalife@eisnet.net

Llama Marketplace, 771 Tucker Road, WiNlock, Washington 98696, (360) 864-8224, e-mail lamrktpl@toledotel.com.

Llamas, Published five times a year. PO Box 250, Jackson, California 95642. Articles, update on conventions, fairs, sales and shows.

The Llama Link, Free monthly publication. P O Box 7907, Kalispell, Montana 59904-7907, (406) 752-2569 or e-mail lamalink.digisys.net. Advertisements for upcoming sales and/or shows, classifieds, sales, maps and display ads.

The Animal Finders Guide, P O Box 99, Prairie Creek, Indiana 47869, (812) 898-2013 or e-mail animalfinder@thnet.com.

And More Information

With advent of the computer the information highway regarding this charming animal offers more and varied information. The following websites include farms, sales and organizations related to the lama species.

Websites: http://www. epnet.com/vintage/llamabanner

	Llama Banner page
animal-magic.com	Araneen Witmer artist
alpacanet.com/	Alpaca Net
addnet.com/llama/	Llamalizer
netride.com./users/jan	Llama owner website
esinet.net./llamas	Llama Life II website
toleotel.com/~lamrktpl/	Llama Marketplace
animalfindersguide.com	The Animal Finders Guide
AlpacaTV.com	Alpacas of Tualatin Valley
surinetwork.org	Suri Network
aob.org	Alpaca Owners & Breeders Assoc.

Llama Veterinarians

With more than 70,000 llamas in North America, veterinarians all over the country are aware of this unique creature. Dr. Murray Fowler of the University of California Davis has written extensively about the llama. Dr. LaRue Johnson of Colorado State University has been noted as another expert in treating these animals. Oregon State University hosts a special llama research program.

Any of the schools and/or the veterinarians are willing share their information with other veterinarians who may not be as well versed in treating the llama.

Wool

This book concentrates primarily on developing a working llama. One of the benefits of training, handling, and grooming is the resulting wool. The yama llama does not produce the best wool in the lama species but some of it can be carded, spun and woven.

Those who plan to utilize the wool will probably choose the alpaca as the best resource. The alpaca's hair is long, crimpy, soft and silky. The alpacas are shorn annually and produce up to 15 pounds of premium fiber. If regularly shorn the hair grows six to eight inches long (15 to 20 cm) each year, but if not clipped the hair can grow as long as 25 inches (63 cm). One of the advantages of the alpaca to some owners is that they need not be groomed. Simply use a blower to keep the fleece clean.

Alpacas come in 22 naturally distinct colors. Their fiber is light and soft to the touch. Yarns spun from alpaca are soft, dense and very warm, especially when the surface is brushed[10].

Llama and alpaca wool continues to grow in popularity and use. Handspinners extol the workability of the llama's long fibrous wool. Due to its' lack of lanolin the fiber is less expensive to process than sheep's wool. The hollow core hair, when spun, is lighter weight than sheep's wool. Although lighter, the llama wool garment will be warmer than a comparable sheep wool garment.

The handcrafter, because of the light weight and texture actually uses less material. The wool's texture ranges from cotton-like to an almost silky smoothness. Lama (alpaca, yama llama, guanaco) wool has historically been priced from $2.00 to $16.00 per ounce depending on quality, length and color.

Spinners and weavers prefer white wool, although alpaca can be easily dyed any color and retain its natural luster. The white wool is easier to dye. Many weavers use the natural red, black or brown coloring of the wool. Llama wool can be felted or woven into beautiful jackets, blankets or ponchos.

When a llama dies some owners will sell the hide to furriers.

---

[10] *Additional reading: FIBRE FACTS and HANDSPINNERS HANDBOOK by Bette Hochberg (Bette & Bernard Hochberg); THE COMPLETE SPINNING BOOK by Candace Crocket (Watson Guptill), SPINNING & WEAVING WITH WOOL by Paula Simmons (Pacific Search Press)*

Manure

Besides being great companions, wonderful pets, and a resource for wool production the pellets a.k.a. manure from the llama makes great fertilizer. Owners sell the pellets by the truckload, by the bag, and have used them in their own gardens with marvelous results. One llama owner after co-opting with other llama owners in his area, developed a marketable *Llamalizer* [11] they retailed in nurseries!

---

[11] *Checkout their website: http:www.addnet.com/llama/ for more information*

9
Troubleshooting

During training the llama may exhibit some undesirable behaviors like spitting or lying down at the wrong time. Following are some general training tips should these situations arise.

Spitting: Yes, llamas do spit. They spit to protect their young and their food. Llamas spit when stressed. The first attempts at grooming may warrant some spitting, kicking and shoving. Regular brushing enables the llama to learn these are unacceptable behaviors.

Do *not* over discipline. Whips, switches, cattle prods or other means of discipline are not required to train these animals. Llamas are gentle creatures and respond to a gentle hand.

Just saying *"No!"* in a loud, angry voice is one effective method to stop spitting. The animal should know you are displeased by your voice and manner. If necessary, give a quick jerk on the halter when you say, "No" or shake your finger near their eye. A camel trainer moves his hand up to the camel's eye in a stop position to discipline. The same hand motion works well with llamas.

After the reprimand, continue with the original activity that caused the animal to become stressed. Praise the animal often. As the llama quiets down, move to the trouble area, while continuing to praise. If spitting occurs, repeat the reprimand and the above process.

This method is not an instant cure. However, it does keep the trainer in charge of the situation. Patience, consistency and gentleness training eventually reward the trainer with a well behaved, responsive llama.

Lying Down On The Trail and Will Not Move: First check the animal thoroughly in case of a physical problem. Check for equipment failure, environmental problems, and medical illness before suspecting the animal is testing authority.

If it is a battle of wills, hold the lead rope and walk towards the tail of the llama. Gently pull the head and neck toward the tail creating some discomfort for the animal. The llama should get up. Upon rising walk in a different direction, if possible, proceed along the previous path.

Lays Down Again: Be sure the llama is not breathing heavily. Be certain the animal is in good physical health. That aside, you may have an animal who is testing your authority. If possible have someone clap her hands near the llama's tail. The person may have to touch the tail to get the llama to stand.

Touching the tail is mimicking natural llama behavior. Llamas fight by chasing and trying to bite the testicles. A llama notices when someone or something is behind him and moves accordingly.

Watch your llama's body language; it may be time for a rest.

If this is not the case, you may want to become more aggressive and pinch *only* the skin near the testicles. The llama should launch forward and move quickly. Be sure to have the lead rope securely in hand.

If you are using a packstring, tie the lazy male to a proven packer. The proven packer will not allow a llama tied behind to lag. The proven male will give ear warnings. Should this prove ineffective, the leader may give a vocal warning and/or a greening as well.

Kushing: Although a cute trick, kushing can be overdone. A working animal needs to stand. When tired or confused the animal may kush in order to please you. When training to kush consider the kind of message you transmit.

Kushing to End a Dispute: Use kushing when you and your animal are in a dispute and you are losing. Llamas fight this way by nature. When you get him down, keep him down for a few moments and shame him with "bad llama." You should notice a change in attitude upon rising. *As the trainer you must always win.*

Fear of Dogs: Dogs are a natural predator. The llama will alert the herd when a dog is seen. Slowly expose the animal to the family's or friend's *friendly* dogs. Do not insist the llama become friendly with every dog. In this way the llama will be alert for strange dogs, but not fear the family pet.

Fear of Water: Llamas, like most animals, will drink from only still water. On the trail you will probably encounter creeks or rivers which need to be forged. Introduce the llama to moving water slowly. Walk him near it. Get his feet wet, then slowly the rest of his body. As the animal gets used to the moving water walk him through it. It is possible to eventually take him swimming in the river.

Fear of Leg Touching: Conditioning is the key. Even ticklish humans can overcome the sensation with consistent touching. Brush the llama's legs gently. Pat him gently down the leg. Use a blower on his legs. If he is a pack animal, let the tie strings dangle from the pack frame. Once he learns he is not in danger he will ignore the action.

Fear of Unknown: When a llama comes across something he is unfamiliar with, he will probably give an alert cry as a warning. The more exposure and experience the animal has the better adjusted he will become to his environment.

Open Mouth Breathing: This may indicate several things: the animal is tired, out of shape, is airing his mouth after spitting, or is suffering from the beginning of hypothermia.

Open mouth breathing generally is not good. If is occurs while packing, pause and let the animal rest. This could also mean your animal is out of condition or overweight.

The llama may be overheating. Remember grooming will get rid of the dead wool. An overabundance of wool may cause the core temperature to rise.

Working llamas who are sheared in the early spring seem to double their stamina for the trail.

Another reason for open mouth on the trail could be over packing the animal. Llamas, like humans, need to build up slowly to their maximum pack weight. Increase the pack weights gradually. A llama who learns to pack 35 pounds the first trip out, will be able to pack more the second. Remember the first day on the trail, as with any exercise program, is always the hardest. Expect daily improvement, but keep your expectations and your increments reasonable.

White Foam at the Mouth: White foam is not always indicative of a major problem. If the foaming is coupled with staggering and dropping to the ground, the animal may be suffering from heat stress. Wet the neck and underbelly immediately. Get the animal cooled down as quickly as possible.

These symptoms are also indicative of ingestion of poisonous plants. Keep a thermometer in your pack to tell the difference.

Green Foam at the Mouth: Call the veterinarian immediately.

Foot Rot: Broken nails allow bacteria to enter and breed infections. Antitoxins give immediate protection. The annual tetanus toxoid vaccine allows for long acting protection.

Inspect nails before a hike to avoid problems with infection. A broken nail should be treated. It can be painful for the animal, causing limping. Examine the hoof for heat and swelling. Call the local veterinarian for remedies.

Appears Ill: Llamas are stoic by nature. If a llama's behavior changes suddenly—lying down more frequently or off his feed, the llama may be ill. Examine for external injuries. Be sure to consult the local veterinarian.

Defanging: Most llama owners defang at about two years of age. The male llama is usually anesthetized while the vet saws off the fangs. This is also an excellent time to heavily groom the llama—taking out mats or dead wool. He will wake up with no negative association with you or the vet.

INDEX

Kopacetic inK presents other books by Dr. Linda Beattie:

MAKING SOAP for FUN and PROFIT

Craft, Hobby, How to

Linda Inlow

ISBN 0-9619634-2-5   Retail: $14.95

80 pages, Index, otabind, laminate cover

Simple step-by-step instructions to make more than 40 different soaps using basic kitchen ingredients, herbs and essential oils. The author also shares some guidelines in turning a hobby into a business.

THE ODD LOT: Raising Unusual Animals

Animals, Pets, Zoology

Dr. Beattie Inlow

ISBN 0-9619637-5-X   Retail: $17.50

112 pages, Index, photos

The ODD Lot contains research and interviews with owners of a wide variety of animals including ratites, miniatures, kangaroos and lamas. It offers history, description and care of these animals as well as resources, web sites, organizations, and owners' personal reflections and advice.

SPECIAL DISCOUNTS AVAILABLE!

TITLE	RETAIL	QUANTITY	SPECIAL	TOTAL
Making Soap for FUN and Profit	$14.95		$12.00	
The ODD LOT	$17.00		$14.00	
Making the Most of Your Llama	$17.95		$14.00	
			SHIPPING & HANDLING	FREE
			Total	

Make Checks or Money Orders payable to Kopacetic inK
and mail to PO Box 323, Kalama, WA 98625
or fax your order (360) 673-1743

Be sure to visit our website **www.goodbooksink.com** for more specials!

Thank you for your purchase of a Kopacetic inK publication.

Printing Books for a Better Tomorrow